Lev Vygotsky's Theory of Cognitive Development: A Simple Guide

A Simple Guide

Dr. Milos Kankaras

Published by Dr. Milos Kankaras, 2023.

Lev Vygotsky: Theory of Cognitive Development

I. Introduction

Lev Vygotsky: the person

Lev Vygotsky was a fascinating and enigmatic figure whose work has had a profound impact on the field of developmental psychology. Born in 1896 in Orsha, a small town in Belarus, Vigotsky grew up in a multilingual family that valued intellectual pursuits. As a child, he was known for his insatiable curiosity and his love of learning, which he pursued with a passion throughout his life.

Vigotsky was a complex and somewhat contradictory figure, known for his charm, wit, and keen intellect, but also for his often fiery temper and his tendency to challenge authority. Despite these quirks, he was a deeply committed scholar who spent his life exploring the mysteries of the human mind.

Throughout his career, Vigotsky was deeply interested in the ways in which cultural and social factors shape cognitive development. He believed that the acquisition of knowledge is a collaborative process, in which individuals engage in dialogue with others in order to learn and grow.

Despite his brilliance, Vigotsky's life was cut tragically short. He died of tuberculosis in 1934, at the age of just 37, leaving behind a legacy of groundbreaking research that continues to influence scholars and researchers around the world today. Despite his brief life, Vigotsky remains one of the most important and influential thinkers in the history of psychology, and his work continues to inspire and inform new generations of scholars and researchers in the field.

Rediscovery and influence

Lev Vygotsky's work has had a profound impact on the fields of psychology, education, and even linguistics. Although his ideas were largely forgotten in the West after his death in 1934, they were rediscovered in the 1960s and 1970s. They have since become widely recognized as some of the most influential and groundbreaking theories in the study of cognitive development.

Throughout his life, Vigotsky was fascinated by the idea of how people learn and develop, and he spent many years studying the way that language, culture, and social interaction all contribute to this process. His work focused on the idea that children learn not only through direct instruction, but also through the culture and language that surrounds them.

One of Vigotsky's most important contributions to the field of psychology was his theory of the "zone of proximal development." According to this theory, children are able to learn best when they are working just beyond the level of what they can do on their own. This means that they are challenged, but not overwhelmed, and that they receive the guidance and support that they need in order to succeed.

Vigotsky's work also had a significant impact on the field of education. His ideas about the importance of social interaction and cultural context in learning have influenced many educational theorists, and his focus on the importance of play and exploration has helped to shape modern ideas about how children learn and develop.

Overall, Vygotsky's work has had a profound impact on the field of psychology, particularly in the areas of cognitive development and education. His theories have been widely studied and applied in a range of settings, from schools to healthcare to business, and continue to shape our understanding of how humans learn and develop.

Key concepts

L ev Vygotsky's theory of cognitive development is based on the premise that social interactions play a critical role in the development of a child's cognitive abilities. According to Vygotsky, a child's development is not simply a matter of maturation, but rather it is shaped by their experiences and interactions with the social and cultural environment. In this section, we will discuss the key concepts of Vygotsky's theory of cognitive development.

Zone of Proximal Development (ZPD): The ZPD refers to the range of tasks that a child can perform with the guidance and support of an adult or more knowledgeable peer. Vygotsky believed that the ZPD represents the area where the most effective learning occurs. By providing appropriate levels of support and challenge within the ZPD, an adult can help a child to achieve a higher level of understanding and mastery of a task.

Example: Imagine a child who is learning to ride a bike. If the child is left completely on their own, they may struggle and may not be able to learn how to ride the bike. However, if an adult or older sibling provides some guidance and support, the child will be able to ride the bike more easily. This is an example of the ZPD, where the child is able to learn and achieve more with the help of a more knowledgeable other.

Scaffolding: Scaffolding is the process of providing temporary support to a child while they are learning a new task or skill. Scaffolding can take many forms, such as breaking a task down into smaller steps, modeling the task, providing feedback, and asking questions. The goal of scaffolding is to gradually transfer responsibility for the task from the adult to the child, as the child becomes more competent.

Example: Continuing with the example of the child learning to ride a bike, the adult or older sibling providing guidance and support can be seen as scaffolding. Just like a scaffold provides support for a building under construction, the adult provides support to the child as they learn to ride the bike. As the child becomes more competent, the adult can gradually withdraw their support until the child is able to ride the bike independently.

Private Speech: Vygotsky observed that children often talk to themselves as they perform tasks, especially in the early stages of learning. He referred to this as private speech, and he believed that it played an important role in cognitive development. Private speech helps children to regulate their behavior, plan and problem-solve, and to internalize language and concepts.

Example: a child playing with blocks might say to themselves, "I'm going to build a tall tower." This private speech is a way for the child to regulate their own behavior and thoughts, and helps them to complete the task successfully.

Cultural Tools: Vygotsky emphasized the importance of cultural tools, such as language, symbols, and other artifacts, in cognitive development. He believed that these tools are used to mediate between the individual and their environment, and that they are acquired through social interactions and cultural practices.

Example: a child learning to read and write might use books, pencils, and paper as cultural tools. These tools are part of the child's cultural environment and are essential for their learning and development.

Social Interaction: Social interaction is a fundamental aspect of Vygotsky's theory. He believed that social interaction is the primary means by which children learn and develop, and that it is through social interactions that children are exposed to new ideas, concepts, and ways of thinking.

Example: A classroom where students are encouraged to engage with one another in conversation, rather than always relying on the teacher for guidance and answers.

Collaborative Learning: Collaborative learning refers to the process of working together with others to achieve a shared goal. Vygotsky believed that collaborative learning is an effective way to promote cognitive development, as it allows children to share their ideas, learn from one another, and build on each other's knowledge.

Example: A group of students working together to create a presentation on a particular topic, with each member taking on a different aspect of the project.

Higher Order Thinking: Vygotsky's theory emphasizes the importance of higher order thinking skills, such as problem-solving, critical thinking, and metacognition. He believed that these skills are developed through social interactions and cultural practices, and that they play a critical role in cognitive development.

Example: A student analyzing a piece of literature and drawing connections to their own life experiences and the broader world or a student developing an argument and supporting it with evidence, using logic and reasoning to persuade others of their point of view.

Mediation: Mediation refers to the role that tools and signs play in children's learning and development. These tools and signs can be physical, such as a calculator or a map, or symbolic, such as a language or a mathematical notation. According to Vygotsky, these tools and signs help to mediate children's understanding of the world and allow them to perform tasks that they would not be able to do otherwise. An example of mediation might be a child using a calculator to solve a complex math problem.

Example: An example of mediation in action is a child learning to ride a bicycle with the help of training wheels. The training wheels act as a mediator by providing support and stability, allowing the child to gradually develop their balance and coordination. As the child gains more confidence and skill, the training wheels can be gradually removed, and the child can ride the bicycle independently.

Social constructivism: Social constructivism is the idea that learning is a social activity that is influenced by culture and social interactions. According to Vygotsky, children learn through social interactions with more knowledgeable others who can provide guidance and support. These interactions help to scaffold children's learning and development and allow them to gradually take on more complex tasks. An example of social constructivism might be a child learning how to play a game with the help of a parent or older sibling.

Example: An example of social constructivism is a classroom discussion where students actively participate in constructing knowledge together. Imagine a history class discussing a historical event. Through dialogue and sharing of perspectives, students build a collective understanding of the event, challenging and refining each other's ideas. They construct new knowledge through social interaction, incorporating diverse viewpoints and constructing a richer understanding of the topic.

Apprenticeship: Apprenticeship is a form of learning in which children learn through observation and participation in a skilled activity. According to Vygotsky, apprenticeship is a powerful way for children to learn because it allows them to observe and learn from skilled practitioners. In an apprenticeship, children gradually take on more responsibility and become more skilled themselves. An example of apprenticeship might be a child learning how to cook with the help of a grandparent or family member.

Example: An example of apprenticeship is a novice woodworker learning from a master craftsman. The apprentice observes the master's techniques, receives guidance, and gradually takes on more complex tasks. The master demonstrates and explains various woodworking techniques, provides feedback, and offers opportunities for the apprentice to practice and refine their skills. Over time, the apprentice gains expertise and becomes proficient in the craft through hands-on learning within the apprenticeship relationship.

Research approach

L ev Vygotsky's method of research and approach to empirical research played a critical role in his development of cognitive development theory. One of Vygotsky's most important insights was that cognitive development cannot be understood in isolation from the social and cultural contexts in which it occurs. He believed that children's development is shaped by their interactions with others, including parents, teachers, and peers. In order to better understand these complex social and cultural factors, Vygotsky developed a unique method of research that he called "experimental-genetic."

Experimental-genetic research involves observing a particular phenomenon over time and studying the ways in which it develops and changes. This approach emphasizes the importance of studying children in their natural environments and tracking changes over time. Vygotsky was particularly interested in studying children's language development, and he used this method to track the way in which children learn to use language and understand the meaning of words.

One of Vygotsky's most famous experiments involved studying children's ability to solve problems with the help of others. In this experiment, Vygotsky presented children with a problem that was too difficult for them to solve on their own. However, when the children were given assistance from an adult or more knowledgeable peer, they were able to successfully solve the problem. This experiment demonstrated the importance of social interaction and collaboration in cognitive development.

Another important aspect of Vygotsky's research was his use of qualitative data. Vygotsky believed that it was important to study children's subjective experiences and to understand the meanings that they attach to their experiences. To this end, he often used interviews and other qualitative methods to gather data about children's thinking and reasoning.

Overall, Vygotsky's approach to research was characterized by a focus on the complex social and cultural factors that shape cognitive development. His experimental-genetic method allowed him to track changes over time and to gain insights into the ways in which children learn and grow. His emphasis on qualitative data helped to deepen our understanding of children's subjective experiences and the meanings that they attach to their experiences. Despite his groundbreaking work, Vygotsky's ideas were largely forgotten in the West until the 1960s, when they were rediscovered and began to have a major impact on the fields of psychology, education, and beyond.

II. The Role of Culture and Social Interaction in Cognitive Development

Culture and social interaction as essential components of cognitive development

In Lev Vygotsky's theory of cognitive development, the role of the cultural environment plays a crucial part in shaping an individual's development. Vygotsky believed that culture is a dynamic and ever-changing system that interacts with individuals, shaping their beliefs, attitudes, and behaviors. He emphasized the importance of culture in the development of higher cognitive processes, such as language, problem-solving, and critical thinking.

Vygotsky believed that the cultural environment, including language and social norms, is transmitted through social interaction. Social interaction creates a zone of proximal development, which is the difference between what an individual can achieve independently and what they can achieve with guidance and support from more knowledgeable others. Vygotsky argued that the cultural environment, which includes tools, symbols, and practices, mediates social interaction and shapes an individual's cognitive development.

Vygotsky's theory of cultural-historical psychology suggests that cultural artifacts, such as books, tools, and technology, are extensions of human cognition. These cultural artifacts enable individuals to think and solve problems in ways that would not be possible without them. For example, the invention of the printing press allowed for the widespread dissemination of knowledge, and the development of computers has revolutionized the way we communicate and solve problems.

In addition, Vygotsky emphasized the importance of the social context in which learning takes place. He believed that social interaction and collaboration are critical for cognitive development. The social environment provides opportunities for individuals to learn from others, exchange ideas, and engage in problem-solving activities. Through social interaction, individuals learn to use cultural tools, symbols, and practices to communicate and solve problems.

Vygotsky also highlighted the role of the family and community in shaping an individual's cognitive development. He believed that cultural artifacts and practices are passed down through generations and that families and communities play a significant role in transmitting cultural knowledge. For example, the traditions and practices of a particular cultural group are learned from family members and other members of the community.

Furthermore, Vygotsky argued that the cultural environment influences an individual's learning and development through language. Language is a tool for communication and problem-solving, and it plays a critical role in shaping an individual's cognitive development. Vygotsky believed that language is learned through social interaction and that it is a mediator of cognitive development.

To illustrate his ideas, Vygotsky used the example of children learning to count. He argued that children initially learn to count through social interactions with adults, who provide the scaffolding they need to understand the concept of numbers. As children progress in their learning, they internalize the knowledge and skills they have acquired, and eventually become capable of counting on their own. Vygotsky also believed that cultural factors, such as the way numbers are represented in different languages, can influence how children learn to count.

Zone of Proximal Development (ZPD) and its role in cognitive development

According to Lev Vygotsky's theory of cognitive development, the Zone of Proximal Development (ZPD) is a crucial concept in the process of learning. The ZPD is the distance between a learner's current level of knowledge and their potential level of knowledge with the help of a more knowledgeable other, such as a teacher, parent, or peer. Vygotsky believed that the ZPD is where learning occurs most effectively.

The ZPD is often illustrated as a scaffold or bridge between what a learner already knows and what they have the potential to learn. The role of the more knowledgeable other is to provide support and guidance to the learner in this zone, allowing them to gradually move towards higher levels of knowledge and understanding.

For example, imagine a child who is learning to read. Their current level of knowledge may be limited to recognizing a few letters and simple words. However, with the help of a teacher or parent, they can begin to read more complex words and sentences that are just beyond their current level of ability. Over time, as they continue to receive support and guidance, they will eventually be able to read independently at a higher level.

Vygotsky believed that the ZPD was an essential component of learning, as it allowed for the development of new skills and knowledge that would not be possible without the help of others. He also believed that the ZPD was dynamic and could change over time as the learner's knowledge and understanding increased.

Another important aspect of the ZPD is that it emphasizes the importance of social interaction in learning. Vygotsky believed that social interaction was necessary for cognitive development to occur, and that learning was a social process that involved collaboration and cooperation between learners and more knowledgeable others.

For example, imagine a group of students working on a science project together. Through their discussions and interactions, they are able to build on each other's ideas and develop a deeper understanding of the topic than they would have been able to achieve on their own. By working together in this way, they are able to expand their ZPD and move towards higher levels of knowledge and understanding.

Vygotsky's concept of the Zone of Proximal Development highlights the importance of social interaction and collaboration in the process of learning. By providing learners with the support and guidance they need to move towards higher levels of knowledge and understanding, the ZPD allows for the development of new skills and knowledge that would not be possible without the help of others. Ultimately, Vygotsky's theory emphasizes the crucial role of social interaction in cognitive development and underscores the importance of collaboration and cooperation in the learning process.

Scaffolding and its importance in cognitive development

Scaffolding is a term coined by Lev Vygotsky that refers to the process of providing support to a learner as they move through a task or problem. It is a way of helping the learner to gradually move towards greater levels of independence and mastery of the task or problem.

The concept of scaffolding is closely linked to Vygotsky's idea of the Zone of Proximal Development (ZPD), which is the range of tasks that a learner can accomplish with the help of a more knowledgeable other (MKO). The MKO can be a teacher, parent, or peer who has greater knowledge or expertise in a particular area than the learner.

Scaffolding involves the MKO providing support to the learner that is tailored to their current level of understanding and ability. The support can take many forms, including asking questions, providing hints, modeling problem-solving strategies, breaking the task into smaller parts, and providing feedback.

The goal of scaffolding is to gradually remove the support as the learner becomes more competent and confident in completing the task on their own. This process of fading support is often referred to as "gradual release."

Scaffolding is an important part of cognitive development because it provides learners with the support they need to move beyond their current level of understanding and ability. It also helps learners to develop metacognitive skills, such as self-regulation and reflection, as they become more aware of their own thinking processes.

One example of scaffolding in action is in the classroom. A teacher might provide a graphic organizer or outline to help students organize their thoughts before writing an essay. The teacher might then model how to use the organizer, asking questions and providing guidance as needed. As students become more proficient with the organizer, the teacher might gradually remove the support until the students are able to use the organizer independently.

Another example of scaffolding is in parent-child interactions. A parent might help a child learn to tie their shoes by breaking the task down into smaller steps and modeling each step for the child. As the child becomes more proficient, the parent might provide less support until the child is able to tie their shoes on their own.

Scaffolding is also an important part of the apprenticeship, where learners work alongside a more experienced practitioner to learn a skill or trade. The experienced practitioner provides guidance and support to the learner, gradually allowing them to take on more responsibility and independence as they develop their skills.

III. Language and Thought in Vygotsky's Theory

Language as a critical tool in cognitive development

Lev Vygotsky viewed language as a critical tool in cognitive development, believing that it plays a fundamental role in shaping the way we think and learn. Vygotsky's theory of cognitive development, often referred to as the sociocultural theory, argues that language is not simply a means of communicating information, but rather a complex and dynamic system that influences all aspects of our cognitive processes.

According to Vygotsky, language enables us to go beyond our innate cognitive abilities and learn from others. Through communication with those around us, we are able to acquire new knowledge and skills that would otherwise be beyond our reach. This process of learning from others is known as social learning, and it is seen as a fundamental part of cognitive development.

Vygotsky also believed that language plays an important role in the development of thinking and problem-solving skills. He argued that the use of language encourages the development of higher-order thinking, such as the ability to reason, plan, and reflect. By using language to explore and discuss ideas, children are able to develop a more sophisticated understanding of the world around them.

Furthermore, Vygotsky viewed language as a means of mediating between the individual and the social world. Through language, we are able to express our thoughts, feelings, and experiences to others, which in turn shapes our understanding of ourselves and our place in society. In this sense, language is seen as a tool for constructing meaning and making sense of the world around us.

To illustrate the importance of language in cognitive development, consider the example of a child learning to solve a puzzle. When working on the puzzle alone, the child may struggle to figure out how to fit the pieces together. However, with the help of an adult or more knowledgeable peer, the child is able to receive guidance and support, which enables them to complete the puzzle more easily. Through the use of language, the child is able to communicate with their mentor and receive feedback and guidance that enables them to move beyond their current level of understanding.

Similarly, consider the example of a child learning a new language. By listening to and interacting with native speakers of the language, the child is able to acquire new vocabulary and grammatical structures that would be difficult to learn through formal instruction alone. Through social interaction and the use of language, the child is able to expand their understanding of the language and develop new cognitive abilities.

Private speech and its role in self-regulation and problem-solving

Private speech, also known as self-talk, refers to the internal dialogue that individuals engage in by talking to themselves. It is a key concept in Vygotsky's theory of cognitive development and plays a crucial role in self-regulation and problem-solving.

Vygotsky believed that private speech develops in early childhood and gradually transforms from external speech to internal thought. At first, children might talk aloud as they engage in activities, such as playing or completing tasks. Over time, this speech becomes internalized, and children begin to use it silently as a means of guiding their actions and thoughts.

While private speech may appear to be nonsensical babbling to an observer, it serves important functions in children's cognitive development. One of the primary functions of private speech is self-regulation. By talking to themselves, children can guide their behavior, manage their emotions, and control their attention. For example, a child might say, "I need to focus and finish this task" or "Take a deep breath, calm down" to regulate their behavior and emotions.

Private speech also plays a significant role in problem-solving. When facing a challenging task, individuals often use private speech to plan, strategize, and evaluate their progress. By talking through the steps aloud or silently, individuals can organize their thoughts and develop effective problem-solving strategies. For instance, a student might say, "First, I need to read the question carefully, then analyze the problem, and finally choose the appropriate solution."

Real-life examples of private speech can be observed in various settings. In a classroom, a student might be working on a difficult math problem and silently talking through the steps, reminding themselves of the relevant formulas or strategies. Similarly, a child engaged in pretend play might engage in private speech, creating narratives and dialogues for their imaginary characters.

Research has shown that private speech is not only a byproduct of cognitive development but also a powerful tool that aids learning and problem-solving. In a classic study by Vygotsky, children were presented with a complex puzzle. Some children were encouraged to verbalize their thoughts while others were asked to remain silent. The results revealed that the children who engaged in private speech were more successful in solving the puzzle compared to those who remained silent.

Private speech is not limited to childhood; it continues to play a role in adult cognitive processes. Even though adults tend to use private speech internally, they still benefit from its self-regulatory and problem-solving functions. For instance, an adult might silently repeat key points during a presentation to stay focused or talk themselves through a challenging task to strategize and overcome obstacles.

It is important to note that private speech is not a sign of cognitive immaturity or a developmental delay. On the contrary, it reflects the active engagement of individuals in their own thinking processes. Encouraging children to engage in private speech can enhance their self-regulation skills and promote effective problem-solving abilities.

Teachers and parents can support the development of private speech by creating a safe and supportive environment where children feel comfortable expressing their thoughts aloud. They can model the use of private speech themselves and encourage children to articulate their thinking processes during activities and tasks. By embracing and valuing private speech, educators and caregivers empower children to become active participants in their own learning and development.

Interconnections between language and thought

Language and thought are intimately interconnected in Vygotsky's theory of cognitive development. According to Vygotsky, language is not simply a means of communication but also a powerful tool that shapes our thinking, perception, and understanding of the world. In this subsection, we will explore the interplay between language and thought, examining how language influences our cognitive processes and how our thoughts shape the way we use language.

Vygotsky believed that language is the primary means through which we develop and express our thoughts. Language allows us to conceptualize abstract ideas, label objects and concepts, and engage in higher-order thinking. It enables us to share our thoughts with others, engage in complex reasoning, and construct meaning from our experiences.

One way in which language influences thought is through its role in organizing and categorizing our knowledge. Language provides us with labels, concepts, and categories that help us make sense of the world. For example, the word "dog" represents a category that encompasses various breeds and individual dogs. By using this word, we can easily refer to and communicate about dogs as a group, making it easier for us to process and understand information related to dogs.

Language also plays a critical role in shaping our perception of the world. Vygotsky argued that language not only reflects our thoughts but also guides and influences our perception. Through language, we develop cognitive schemas and frameworks that help us interpret and make sense of our experiences. For example, language allows us to perceive an object not just as a physical entity but also as a member of a particular category with specific attributes. By using language to label and describe objects, we can mentally organize and make sense of our surroundings.

Furthermore, language facilitates higher-order thinking and problem-solving. Through the use of language, we can engage in internal dialogue, also known as private speech, where we talk to ourselves to regulate our thoughts and actions. This self-talk allows us to plan, evaluate, and reflect on our thinking processes, enabling us to solve problems more effectively. For instance, a student may use self-talk to guide their reasoning while solving a complex math problem, saying, "Let me break it down into smaller steps" or "What strategy can I use here?"

Real-life examples of the interconnections between language and thought are abundant. Consider a child learning a new language. As they acquire new vocabulary and grammar, their thinking patterns may shift, and they may begin to perceive and conceptualize the world differently through the lens of the new language. Similarly, individuals who are bilingual or multilingual often report experiencing variations in their thought processes depending on the language they are using.

The interplay between language and thought can also be observed in professional contexts. For instance, a scientist uses language to formulate hypotheses, discuss research findings, and communicate complex ideas within their field. By engaging in scientific discourse, they not only share their thoughts but also refine and develop new concepts and theories.

It is essential to note that Vygotsky's theory does not propose that language determines thought or that our thinking is entirely limited by the language we use. Instead, it suggests a dynamic relationship between the two, with language influencing and being influenced by our thoughts and cognitive processes. Language provides a framework for thinking and expressing our thoughts, but our thoughts also shape the way we use language.

IV. The Importance of Play in Cognitive Development

Play as an essential component of cognitive development

Play is a fundamental aspect of childhood that goes beyond mere amusement and entertainment. In Vygotsky's theory of cognitive development, play holds a crucial role in shaping children's thinking, problem-solving abilities, and overall cognitive growth. In this subsection, we will explore the significance of play as an essential component of cognitive development, examining its impact on various cognitive processes and providing real-life examples to illustrate its importance.

Vygotsky believed that play provides a fertile ground for children to actively engage with their environment and learn through firsthand experiences. Through play, children are able to explore, experiment, and make sense of the world around them in a safe and enjoyable manner. It serves as a natural context for them to develop and practice a range of cognitive skills.

One key aspect of play is its ability to foster imaginative thinking and creativity. When engaged in pretend play, children create imaginary scenarios, take on different roles, and invent narratives. This type of play allows them to stretch their imagination, think outside the box, and engage in complex storytelling. For example, when children engage in a pretend tea party, they have to imagine the roles of different characters, plan the sequence of events, and use their creativity to develop the storyline.

Play also facilitates problem-solving and critical thinking skills. During play, children encounter various challenges and obstacles that require them to think flexibly and find solutions. For instance, building with blocks or solving puzzles requires children to plan, strategize, and adapt their actions to achieve their desired outcome. By engaging in play, children develop their problem-solving abilities, learn to overcome difficulties, and become more resourceful thinkers.

Furthermore, play provides opportunities for social interaction and collaboration, which contribute to cognitive development. When children engage in cooperative play, such as building together or participating in group games, they learn to communicate, negotiate, and work towards common goals. Through these social interactions, they develop social cognition, empathy, and an understanding of others' perspectives. For example, when children engage in a pretend grocery store, they must take turns, negotiate prices, and engage in social exchanges, enhancing their social and cognitive skills simultaneously.

Play also supports the development of executive functions, which are essential cognitive processes that facilitate self-regulation and goal-directed behavior. During play, children must organize their thoughts, plan their actions, and inhibit impulsive responses. For instance, when playing a board game, children need to remember the rules, take turns, and make strategic decisions. Through these experiences, they enhance their self-control, attention, and cognitive flexibility.

Real-life examples of play's role in cognitive development can be observed in various contexts. In early childhood classrooms, teachers incorporate play-based learning activities that stimulate children's cognitive growth. For instance, engaging in sensory play with sand or water allows children to explore different textures, observe cause-and-effect relationships, and develop their scientific thinking.

In the digital age, technology-mediated play has also become prevalent. Interactive educational apps or games provide children with opportunities to engage in problem-solving, critical thinking, and collaboration. For example, puzzle-solving games encourage children to think strategically, analyze patterns, and exercise their spatial reasoning skills.

It is important to note that play is not limited to early childhood but continues to play a role in cognitive development throughout the lifespan. Even in adulthood, engaging in activities such as board games, sports, or creative hobbies can enhance cognitive skills, promote social interactions, and provide opportunities for personal growth.

Educators and parents can foster play-based learning environments that promote cognitive development. They can provide open-ended materials and encourage imaginative play, create opportunities for collaborative play, and support the integration of play into educational settings. By recognizing the importance of play and its role in cognitive development, we can nurture children's curiosity, creativity, problem-solving skills, and social-emotional development.

The concept of "play with rules"

Play is a multifaceted activity that encompasses various forms, one of which is "play with rules." This type of play involves engaging in activities that have predetermined rules and structures, such as organized games, sports, and board games. In this subsection, we will explore the concept of "play with rules" and its significant role in cognitive development, highlighting its impact on skills like problem-solving, social interaction, and self-regulation. Through real-life examples, we will illustrate how this type of play enhances cognitive growth and fosters essential abilities.

"Play with rules" provides a structured framework for children to navigate and engage in social interactions. By participating in games with established rules, children learn to follow guidelines, take turns, and adhere to predetermined boundaries. These rules set the foundation for social interactions, promoting cooperation, fairness, and respect for others. For example, in a game of soccer, players must follow specific rules regarding dribbling, passing, and scoring. By adhering to these rules, children learn to cooperate with their teammates, communicate effectively, and engage in fair play.

One of the key cognitive benefits of "play with rules" is the development of problem-solving skills. When children participate in games, they encounter challenges and obstacles that require them to strategize, think critically, and make decisions under pressure. They need to anticipate their opponents' moves, evaluate various options, and adjust their strategies accordingly. For instance, in a game of chess, players must analyze the positions of different pieces, plan their moves, and anticipate their opponents' responses. Through this process, children develop their logical reasoning, spatial awareness, and problem-solving abilities.

Furthermore, "play with rules" promotes self-regulation, as children must control their impulses, manage their emotions, and follow the established rules of the game. They learn to regulate their behavior, take turns, and accept the outcomes of the game, whether they win or lose. This type of play fosters self-control, resilience, and emotional regulation. For example, when playing a card game, children must resist the temptation to cheat or become frustrated when their hand is not favorable. By engaging in "play with rules," children develop important life skills related to self-regulation and emotional intelligence.

Real-life examples of "play with rules" can be seen in various settings. In school, organized sports activities allow children to engage in structured play, developing teamwork, sportsmanship, and problem-solving skills. For instance, a game of basketball requires players to follow the rules, work collaboratively, and strategize their moves to outwit the opposing team.

Board games also provide opportunities for "play with rules." Games like Monopoly, Scrabble, or Settlers of Catan require players to follow specific rules, make strategic decisions, and adapt their gameplay based on the actions of others. These games enhance critical thinking, mathematical skills, and negotiation abilities.

Even traditional childhood games like tag, hide-and-seek, or Simon says involve "play with rules." These games introduce children to the concept of rules and provide opportunities for social interaction, cooperation, and problem-solving within the context of play.

Educators and parents can support the development of cognitive skills through "play with rules" by introducing age-appropriate games and activities. By providing opportunities for children to engage in organized play, they promote social skills, strategic thinking, and self-regulation. They can also foster a sense of fairness and respect by ensuring that the rules are followed and encouraging positive sportsmanship.

Benefits of imaginative play

Imaginative play, also known as pretend play or fantasy play, is a rich and vibrant form of play that holds immense importance in children's cognitive development. In this subsection, we will explore the benefits of imaginative play and its close relationship to cognitive growth, highlighting its impact on creativity, problem-solving, language development, and social skills. Through real-life examples, we will illustrate how imaginative play nurtures children's cognitive abilities and fosters their overall development.

One of the significant benefits of imaginative play is its promotion of creativity and divergent thinking. When engaged in pretend play, children have the freedom to create and explore imaginative scenarios, taking on various roles and inventing narratives. They can be superheroes, doctors, teachers, or any character they desire. Through this process, children exercise their creative thinking skills, expanding their imaginations and exploring alternative possibilities. For example, a child engaged in imaginative play may transform a cardboard box into a spaceship and embark on an intergalactic adventure, using their creativity to invent new storylines and solve imaginary challenges.

Imaginative play also nurtures problem-solving abilities. During pretend play, children encounter situations that require them to think critically, make decisions, and solve problems. They engage in complex problem-solving within the context of their play narratives. For instance, when playing "restaurant," children must determine the menu, take orders, and solve issues that arise during the pretend dining experience.

By engaging in imaginative play, children learn to think flexibly, generate solutions, and develop problem-solving strategies.

Moreover, imaginative play contributes to language development and communication skills. As children create and act out scenarios, they engage in verbal and non-verbal communication, expanding their vocabulary, and refining their language abilities. They learn to express themselves, negotiate roles and plotlines, and engage in conversations with their playmates. For instance, when playing "doctor," children may use medical terminology, engage in dialogues with their patients, and practice their communication skills. Through imaginative play, children enhance their language comprehension, expressive abilities, and social communication skills.

Another critical aspect of imaginative play is its role in fostering social skills and promoting empathy. When children engage in pretend play, they take on different roles and perspectives, allowing them to understand and empathize with others. They learn to consider the feelings and perspectives of their playmates, practice turn-taking, and engage in cooperative play. For example, when playing "family," children learn to navigate social roles, share responsibilities, and engage in imaginative problem-solving within the context of their make-believe family dynamics.

Real-life examples of imaginative play are abundant and can be observed in various settings. In a classroom, children may engage in a pretend grocery store, taking turns as the shopkeeper and the customer, practicing their math skills as they pretend to exchange money and count items. In a park, children may engage in imaginative play by constructing a pretend fort, assigning different roles, and collaboratively defending their territory. These examples demonstrate how imaginative play transcends cultural boundaries and is a universal form of play that promotes cognitive, social, and emotional development.

Educators and parents can foster imaginative play by providing open-ended materials, such as blocks, dress-up clothes, and art supplies.

They can create imaginative play spaces and encourage children to explore their imaginations freely. Additionally, adults can actively participate in imaginative play, taking on roles and engaging in cooperative narratives with children. By embracing and supporting imaginative play, caregivers and educators provide children with a rich environment that stimulates their cognitive growth, enhances their social skills, and fosters their creativity.

V. Applications of Vygotsky's Theory in Education and Development

Influence of Vygotsky's theory on educational practices

Vygotsky's theory of cognitive development has had a profound impact on educational practices, particularly in the areas of teaching methods and curriculum design. His emphasis on the social and cultural aspects of learning has led to the development of educational approaches that promote collaboration, scaffolding, and the integration of students' cultural backgrounds. In this subsection, we will explore how Vygotsky's theory has influenced educational practices, providing real-life examples to illustrate its application in the classroom.

One key concept derived from Vygotsky's theory is the importance of social interaction and collaboration in the learning process. Vygotsky believed that learning occurs through dialogue and interaction with more knowledgeable others. This idea has influenced teaching methods by emphasizing cooperative learning activities, group discussions, and peer collaboration. For example, in a mathematics class, students may work together to solve complex problems, discuss different strategies, and explain their reasoning to one another. Through these collaborative activities, students not only deepen their understanding of the subject matter but also develop their communication and social skills.

Another aspect of Vygotsky's theory that has influenced educational practices is the concept of scaffolding. Vygotsky proposed that teachers should provide support and guidance to students to help them move beyond their current level of understanding. This support, known as scaffolding, can take various forms, such as providing prompts, asking leading questions, or breaking down complex tasks into manageable steps. For instance, in a writing lesson, a teacher may provide a graphic organizer to help students structure their ideas and provide feedback during the writing process. By providing scaffolding, teachers empower students to tackle more challenging tasks, gradually reducing the support as students become more proficient.

Vygotsky's theory also highlights the importance of the cultural and historical context in which learning takes place. He believed that individuals acquire knowledge and skills through their interactions with their cultural environment. This perspective has led to the recognition of the value of incorporating students' cultural backgrounds and experiences into the curriculum. For example, in a social studies class, teachers may incorporate literature, artifacts, and stories from diverse cultures to enrich students' understanding of different societies and promote cultural appreciation. By incorporating students' cultural backgrounds, educational practices become more inclusive and relevant, fostering a sense of belonging and promoting multicultural understanding.

Furthermore, Vygotsky's theory has influenced curriculum design by emphasizing the zone of proximal development (ZPD). The ZPD refers to the range of tasks that students can accomplish with guidance and support. Educators use the concept of the ZPD to design instructional activities that challenge students while providing the necessary support for success. For example, in a science lesson, teachers may design experiments that are slightly above students' current abilities but within their ZPD. This approach ensures that students are appropriately challenged, fostering growth and maximizing their learning potential.

Real-life examples of Vygotsky's theory in educational practices can be observed in classrooms around the world. In a primary school, students may engage in project-based learning, where they collaborate to solve real-world problems. This approach encourages students to draw on their prior knowledge, work together to find solutions, and develop critical thinking and problem-solving skills. Similarly, in a language class, teachers may employ peer editing strategies, where students provide feedback and support to their classmates in improving their writing skills. This peer interaction enhances students' language development, fosters a sense of community, and promotes active engagement in the learning process.

Vygotsky's theory has also influenced the use of technology in education. Digital tools, such as online discussion forums, collaborative documents, and educational apps, can provide platforms for social interaction, peer collaboration, and knowledge sharing. For instance, students may engage in online discussions about a novel they are reading, sharing their interpretations and exchanging ideas. This digital collaboration enables students to learn from one another, broaden their perspectives, and develop digital literacy skills.

Application to child development and intervention programs

Vygotsky's theory of cognitive development has not only influenced educational practices but also has significant implications for child development and intervention programs. This subsection will explore the application of Vygotsky's theory to child development, focusing on the role of social interaction, scaffolding, and cultural context in fostering optimal growth. Real-life examples will illustrate how these principles can be incorporated into intervention programs to support children's development in various domains.

One key aspect of Vygotsky's theory is the emphasis on social interaction as a catalyst for learning and development. According to Vygotsky, children learn best when they engage in meaningful interactions with more knowledgeable others. This notion has profound implications for intervention programs aimed at supporting children's development. By creating environments that foster positive social interactions, children can engage in joint problem-solving, receive guidance from adults or peers, and expand their cognitive abilities. For instance, in a classroom setting, a teacher may organize small-group activities where children collaborate to complete a task, providing an opportunity for peer interaction and learning from one another.

Scaffolding, another core concept in Vygotsky's theory, plays a crucial role in intervention programs. Scaffolding involves providing temporary support and guidance to a child, allowing them to accomplish tasks that are just beyond their current level of competence. By providing appropriate levels of support, educators and interventionists can facilitate children's learning and help them progress to higher levels of development. For example, in a reading intervention program, a teacher may use guided reading sessions, where they provide support in decoding words, understanding text, and making inferences. This scaffolding gradually fades as the child gains confidence and proficiency in reading independently.

The cultural context is also a vital component of Vygotsky's theory, recognizing that children's development is influenced by the values, beliefs, and practices of their cultural community. Intervention programs that take this into account can better support children's development by respecting and incorporating their cultural backgrounds. For instance, a program designed to enhance language skills may include storytelling activities that draw on the cultural traditions and experiences of the children. By incorporating children's cultural heritage, the intervention program becomes more meaningful and relevant, fostering a sense of identity and promoting cultural pride.

One area where Vygotsky's theory has been applied effectively is in language development interventions. Language is a fundamental aspect of cognitive development, and Vygotsky emphasized the role of social interaction and language in shaping children's thinking. Intervention programs that follow Vygotsky's principles often involve rich language experiences, interactive storytelling, and conversations that scaffold children's language skills. For example, in a preschool language intervention program, teachers may engage children in interactive read-alouds, where they encourage discussions, ask open-ended questions, and model rich vocabulary use. These interactions promote language development, extend children's thinking, and provide opportunities for social and cognitive growth.

Another area where Vygotsky's theory is highly relevant is in the domain of social-emotional development. Vygotsky emphasized the importance of social interaction and collaboration in children's development of self-regulation, empathy, and social skills. Intervention programs can draw on Vygotsky's principles by creating environments that foster positive social interactions, promote emotional understanding, and provide opportunities for cooperative play. For instance, a social-emotional intervention program for young children may involve role-playing activities, where children engage in pretend play scenarios that focus on social problem-solving, perspective-taking, and emotional regulation. Through these activities, children develop crucial social-emotional skills and learn to navigate social interactions effectively.

Furthermore, Vygotsky's theory has implications for interventions aimed at supporting children with special needs or developmental delays. By understanding the zone of proximal development (ZPD), interventionists can tailor their support to meet each child's individual needs. For example, in a therapy session for a child with language delays, the therapist may use strategies such as modeling, prompting, and gradual fading of support to help the child develop their language skills within their ZPD. This approach ensures that the intervention is tailored to the child's specific needs, providing the necessary support while promoting independence and growth.

Real-life examples of Vygotsky's theory in child development and intervention programs can be found across various settings. In a preschool setting, an intervention program for children with autism may focus on social communication skills, incorporating structured play activities that provide opportunities for joint attention, imitation, and turn-taking. In a primary school, a reading intervention program may adopt a peer-tutoring approach, where older students support younger peers in developing reading skills, promoting both academic and social growth.

Criticisms and controversies surrounding Vygotsky's theory

Vygotsky's theory of cognitive development has had a significant impact on our understanding of child development and education. However, like any theoretical framework, it has also faced criticisms and controversies. This subsection will provide an overview of some of the main criticisms raised against Vygotsky's theory, along with the controversies surrounding its application. Real-life examples will be used to illustrate these criticisms and controversies, shedding light on the ongoing debates in the field.

One criticism often directed at Vygotsky's theory is the lack of empirical evidence supporting some of its key concepts. Critics argue that while Vygotsky's ideas are influential and intuitively appealing, there is a need for more empirical research to validate his claims. For example, the concept of the zone of proximal development (ZPD) has been criticized for its subjective nature and difficulty in operationalizing and measuring. Critics contend that without rigorous empirical evidence, Vygotsky's theory may lack the scientific validity necessary for widespread acceptance.

Another criticism concerns the cultural and contextual specificity of Vygotsky's theory. Critics argue that Vygotsky's work was primarily based on studies conducted in Soviet Russia during a specific historical and cultural period. As a result, some argue that the applicability of Vygotsky's ideas to other cultural contexts may be limited. For instance, Vygotsky's emphasis on collective and collaborative learning may not align with cultural values that prioritize individual achievement and competition. Critics contend that Vygotsky's theory needs to be examined and adapted to account for the diverse cultural contexts in which it is applied.

Controversies also surround the implementation of Vygotsky's theory in educational settings. One controversy revolves around the extent to which Vygotsky's ideas should guide instructional practices. Critics argue that while Vygotsky's theory emphasizes social interaction and collaboration, it may not provide clear guidelines for effective teaching methods. For example, the concept of scaffolding is considered subjective, leaving educators uncertain about how much support to provide and when to withdraw it. This lack of clarity has led to debates about the best ways to apply Vygotsky's principles in the classroom.

Additionally, there are concerns about the potential for overreliance on adult guidance and intervention, which may hinder children's independence and problem-solving skills. Critics argue that excessive scaffolding may limit children's opportunities to explore and learn through independent discovery. This controversy highlights the need for a balanced approach that recognizes the importance of both teacher guidance and student autonomy.

Furthermore, Vygotsky's theory has faced criticism for its limited consideration of individual differences in development. Critics argue that Vygotsky's focus on the social and cultural aspects of learning may overlook the unique characteristics and abilities of individual learners. For example, the theory may not adequately account for variations in children's cognitive capacities or learning styles. Critics suggest that a more comprehensive understanding of child development should encompass both social and individual factors.

Real-life examples can provide insights into the criticisms and controversies surrounding Vygotsky's theory. In an educational setting, a teacher may struggle to implement Vygotsky's ideas effectively due to the lack of specific guidelines and the need for individualized instruction. For instance, in a diverse classroom with students from various cultural backgrounds, the teacher may find it challenging to strike a balance between promoting social interaction and respecting individual learning preferences. These challenges highlight the complexities of applying Vygotsky's theory in real-world contexts.

Despite these criticisms and controversies, it is important to recognize the enduring impact of Vygotsky's theory on child development and education. Many educators and researchers continue to find value in his ideas, using them as a framework for understanding the social and cultural dimensions of learning. While Vygotsky's theory may require further refinement and empirical validation, it has undoubtedly contributed to our understanding of the intricate interplay between social interaction, culture, and cognitive development.

VI. Conclusion

Summary of key points in Vygotsky's theory of cognitive development

Throughout this chapter, we have explored the fascinating and influential theory of cognitive development proposed by Lev Vygotsky. His theory offers valuable insights into the role of social interaction, cultural context, language, and play in shaping children's cognitive development. In this subsection, we will summarize the key points of Vygotsky's theory, highlighting its major contributions to our understanding of how children learn and grow.

Social Interaction: Vygotsky emphasized the fundamental role of social interaction in cognitive development. He argued that children learn best through meaningful interactions with more knowledgeable others, such as parents, teachers, and peers. These interactions provide opportunities for learning and guidance, enabling children to acquire new knowledge and skills.

Zone of Proximal Development (ZPD): One of the central concepts in Vygotsky's theory, the ZPD refers to the gap between a child's current level of development and their potential level with assistance. Vygotsky proposed that optimal learning occurs within this zone, where a child can successfully complete tasks with appropriate support and guidance from a more competent individual.

Scaffolding: Vygotsky introduced the concept of scaffolding, which involves providing temporary support and guidance to a child as they engage in learning tasks. Scaffolding enables children to accomplish tasks that they would not be able to complete independently, promoting their cognitive growth and development. As children become more competent, the scaffolding can be gradually reduced to foster greater independence.

Cultural Context: Vygotsky highlighted the critical role of cultural context in cognitive development. He argued that children's learning is deeply influenced by the values, beliefs, and practices of their cultural community. Cultural tools, such as language, symbols, and artifacts, mediate children's understanding of the world and shape their cognitive processes.

Language and Thought: According to Vygotsky, language plays a central role in cognitive development. He viewed language as a tool for thinking and believed that children's thought processes are closely intertwined with their use of language. Through language, children acquire knowledge, engage in problem-solving, and develop higher-order thinking skills.

Private Speech: Vygotsky recognized the importance of private speech, which refers to the self-directed verbalizations that children engage in during problem-solving tasks. He argued that private speech serves as a cognitive tool, aiding children in planning, self-regulation, and problem-solving. Over time, private speech internalizes and becomes inner speech, an internal mental process.

Play and Cognitive Development: Vygotsky emphasized the crucial role of play in cognitive development. He saw play as a context where children can engage in imaginary situations, experiment with different roles, and exercise their cognitive abilities. Through play, children develop problem-solving skills, creativity, and social understanding.

The More Knowledgeable Other: Vygotsky emphasized the importance of the more knowledgeable other, who can be a parent, teacher, or peer, in guiding children's learning. The more knowledgeable other provides support, models desired behaviors, and engages in collaborative problem-solving, facilitating the child's cognitive development.

Cultural-Historical Theory: Vygotsky's theory is often referred to as the cultural-historical theory, as it acknowledges the influence of both cultural and historical factors on children's development. Vygotsky believed that the interplay between culture and individual development is essential in understanding cognitive growth.

Reflection on the legacy and continued relevance of Vygotsky's theory

Vygotsky's theory of cognitive development has had a profound impact on the field of psychology and education, leaving a lasting legacy that continues to shape our understanding of how children learn and develop. In this subsection, we will reflect on the legacy of Vygotsky's theory and its continued relevance in contemporary research and practice.

One of the key contributions of Vygotsky's theory is its emphasis on the social nature of learning. Vygotsky challenged the prevailing view of cognitive development as an individual, internal process and highlighted the crucial role of social interactions in shaping children's thinking. His theory has influenced research on social cognition, emphasizing the importance of social context, cultural influences, and collaborative learning. Researchers continue to explore the ways in which social interactions, peer collaboration, and cooperative learning impact children's cognitive development.

Vygotsky's concept of the Zone of Proximal Development (ZPD) remains a fundamental aspect of his theory. The notion that children can accomplish more with the support of a knowledgeable other has significant implications for educational practices. Educators have embraced the concept of scaffolding, using it to guide instructional strategies that provide targeted support to students as they work within their ZPD. Scaffolding helps students build upon their existing knowledge and skills, fostering their growth and enabling them to achieve higher levels of competence.

The cultural-historical perspective introduced by Vygotsky is another lasting contribution. Vygotsky emphasized the importance of cultural tools, such as language, symbols, and artifacts, in shaping children's cognition. This perspective has influenced research on the impact of cultural context on learning and has highlighted the need to consider diverse cultural backgrounds in educational settings. Vygotsky's recognition of the role of culture in cognitive development has spurred discussions and efforts to create culturally responsive and inclusive learning environments.

Furthermore, Vygotsky's emphasis on the role of language in cognitive development has had a lasting impact on educational practices. Language is not only a means of communication but also a tool for thinking and problem-solving. Educators recognize the importance of fostering language development and providing opportunities for students to engage in meaningful language-rich activities. Vygotsky's theory has influenced instructional strategies that promote language acquisition, dialogue, and collaborative discourse in the classroom.

Vygotsky's theory also sheds light on the significant role of play in cognitive development. Play is not merely a recreational activity but a context where children engage in imaginative and purposeful exploration. Vygotsky recognized that play allows children to create imaginary situations, experiment with different roles, and exercise their cognitive abilities. Play-based approaches have gained recognition in early childhood education, with educators understanding the value of play in fostering problem-solving skills, creativity, and socio-emotional development.

The legacy of Vygotsky's theory extends beyond the field of education. It has influenced diverse areas, such as developmental psychology, cultural psychology, and special education. Vygotsky's ideas have informed research on developmental disorders, language impairments, and learning disabilities. Professionals working with children with special needs have incorporated Vygotsky's principles into intervention programs, recognizing the importance of social interaction and guided participation in supporting their development.

Despite Vygotsky's significant contributions, it is important to acknowledge the ongoing debates and challenges surrounding his theory. Critics have raised valid concerns about the lack of empirical evidence for some aspects of his theory and the cultural specificity of his findings. Additionally, the practical implementation of Vygotsky's ideas in educational settings may present challenges, requiring careful consideration of individual differences, instructional strategies, and cultural contexts.

Suggestions for future research and application of Vygotsky's theory in the field of psychology and education.

Vygotsky's theory of cognitive development has provided valuable insights into the interplay between social interaction, culture, and cognition. However, there is still much to explore and discover within this framework. In this subsection, we will discuss several suggestions for future research and application of Vygotsky's theory in the field of psychology and education.

Further Empirical Research: While Vygotsky's theory has influenced our understanding of cognitive development, there is a need for more empirical research to validate and expand upon his ideas. Future studies can investigate the specific mechanisms through which social interaction influences cognitive processes, explore the cultural variations in the implementation of Vygotsky's principles, and examine the long-term effects of scaffolding and collaborative learning on children's academic achievement.

Cultural Adaptation: Vygotsky's theory originated in a specific cultural and historical context, and its application in diverse cultural settings requires careful consideration. Future research can focus on adapting Vygotsky's concepts to different cultural contexts, recognizing the unique cultural values, practices, and learning environments that may influence children's cognitive development. This cultural adaptation can enhance the applicability and effectiveness of Vygotsky's theory in diverse educational settings.

Individual Differences: Vygotsky's theory emphasizes the role of social interaction in cognitive development, but it is essential to consider individual differences in learning styles, abilities, and needs. Future research can explore how individual differences interact with social interaction, scaffolding, and the ZPD. Understanding how to tailor instructional practices to meet the diverse needs of learners can enhance the effectiveness of Vygotsky-inspired interventions.

Technology and Digital Learning Environments: The emergence of digital technologies and online learning platforms present new opportunities for research and application of Vygotsky's theory. Future studies can explore how technology-mediated social interactions and collaborative learning environments impact cognitive development. Additionally, the use of educational apps, virtual reality, and other digital tools can be investigated to determine how they can effectively scaffold learning and promote higher-order thinking skills.

Cross-disciplinary Collaboration: Vygotsky's theory has implications not only for psychology and education but also for other disciplines such as sociology, anthropology, and neuroscience. Future research can foster cross-disciplinary collaboration to gain a more comprehensive understanding of cognitive development. For example, combining Vygotsky's sociocultural perspective with insights from neuroscience can shed light on the neural mechanisms underlying social interaction and cognitive processes.

Educational Practices and Teacher Training: Vygotsky's theory offers valuable guidance for educational practices, curriculum design, and teacher training. Future research can explore the most effective ways to translate Vygotsky's ideas into practical strategies that support student learning. Additionally, teacher training programs can incorporate Vygotskian principles to equip educators with the knowledge and skills to create classroom environments that foster social interaction, scaffolding, and higher-order thinking.

Parenting and Early Childhood Interventions: Vygotsky's theory has implications for parenting practices and early childhood interventions. Future research can investigate how Vygotskian principles can be applied in home environments to promote children's cognitive development. Additionally, the design and evaluation of early childhood interventions can integrate Vygotsky's concepts to provide children with enriching social interactions and scaffolded learning experiences.

Longitudinal Studies: Long-term studies examining the effects of Vygotskian-inspired interventions can provide valuable insights into the lasting impact of social interaction and scaffolding on cognitive development. These studies can explore how Vygotskian principles contribute to academic achievement, problem-solving abilities, and socio-emotional development over time.

The future research and application of Vygotsky's theory hold great potential to further our understanding of cognitive development and enhance educational practices. By conducting more empirical research, considering cultural adaptations, addressing individual differences, harnessing the power of technology, fostering cross-disciplinary collaboration, improving educational practices and teacher training, focusing on parenting and early childhood interventions, and conducting longitudinal studies, we can continue to build upon Vygotsky's ideas and create environments that optimize children's cognitive growth and learning experiences.

Don't miss out!

Visit the website below and you can sign up to receive emails whenever Dr. Milos Kankaras publishes a new book. There's no charge and no obligation.

https://books2read.com/r/B-A-LEAZ-EAOKC

BOOKS 2 READ

Connecting independent readers to independent writers.

Also by Dr. Milos Kankaras

A Simple Guide

Lev Vygotsky's Theory of Cognitive Development: A Simple Guide

Gender Equality

Domestic Violence: Effectiveness of Intervention Programs

Standalone

Jean Piaget's Theory of Cognitive Development: A Simple Guide

Watch for more at https://oecd.academia.edu/MilošKankaraš.

About the Author

Dr. Miloš Kankaraš is an experienced researcher, policy analyst, and author with a rich track

record in providing an empirical foundation for evidence-based public policy in international settings. He worked in academia before moving to some of the leading international organisations, where he examined issues ranging from education, skill development, social policy, working conditions, gender equality, quality of life, etc. Miloš published extensively in a variety of policy and research areas. He has an undergraduate degree in Psychology, graduate degrees in educational psychology and international social policy, and a PhD in the area of cross-cultural research.

Read more at https://oecd.academia.edu/MilošKankaraš.